An Activity Book for Kids

By Joan Eckstein and Joyce Gleit
Illustrated by Stan Tusan

AN AVON CAMELOT BOOK

FUN WITH MAKING THINGS
is an original publication of Avon Books.
This work has never before appeared in book form.

AVON BOOKS
A division of
The Hearst Corporation
959 Eighth Avenue
New York, New York 10019
Copyright © 1979 by Joan Eckstein and Joyce Gleit
Published by arrangement with the authors.
Library of Congress Catalog Card Number: 78–63604
ISBN: 0–380–43315–X

First Camelot Printing, April, 1979

AVON TRADEMARK REG. U.S. PAT. OFF. AND IN
OTHER COUNTRIES, MARCA REGISTRADA, HECHO EN
U.S.A.

Printed in the U.S.A.

*We dedicate this book to our kids,
Paul, Jonathan, Stefanie, and Lisa,
who kept themselves so busy making things
that we had time to write this book.*

Contents

Game Thing

Plant Things

Things to Do When You're Sick in Bed

Things with Wood and Stuff

Introduction

The crafts in this book are for everyday special occasions. They are for those times when you are sick in bed, or when there is no one to play with. There are things to make when it is raining or snowing and you can't go out to play, or when your mom and dad take you on a trip and you are trapped in a boring hotel. It's for those times when you are feeling creative and can't think of anything to do. This book will show you that there is always something to do. Most of the crafts in this book can be made with easy-to-find items. Things that are found around the house or in your own backyard. On the beach, in the woods, or in a five-and-ten or hardware store. There are no complicated tools to use, and there are step-by-step directions and easy-to-understand illustrations.

Some of the crafts are easier than others. If you decide to make something that seems more complicated, just ask an older person for some help. You can make any of the things in this book by yourself. For instance, you might want to try potato printing or finger puppets to cheer yourself up on a lonely snowy or rainy day. You could collect a bunch of friends and make music with a tin can band. And don't let your mom throw out your old sneakers. Paint them. Decorate them with spangles. Wear them.

And, of course, the best gift you can give someone is something you have made yourself. You can make your best birthday pal a batik shirt or give your grandma a vase you have made from a soda bottle. Mom and Dad will love to have place mats you have woven yourself. You can even make your dog a gift.

Just follow the instructions. But don't feel that you have to be exact. Don't be afraid to use your imagination. If you want to change something or make it a different color and a different material, that is just fine. Don't be afraid to be creative. Your own ideas are fun, and they are you.

Have a good time.

Tin Can Things

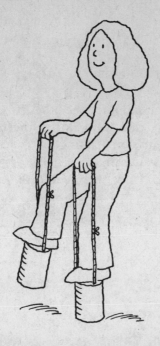

TIN CAN STILTS

**You'll feel 10 feet tall, walking
on stilts you can make in seconds.**

You will need:

1. Two large, empty juice cans, the 46-ounce size. Cans should be intact, tops and bottoms on, except for the 2 holes on top for pouring out the juice.
2. Two pieces of heavy cord or rope. The length should be about 2 times your measurement from waist to heels.

What to do:

1. Thread one end of the cord or rope into one hole of a can and out the other.
2. Knot the ends of the cord together, making a big loop of cord.
3. Repeat steps 1 and 2 for the other stilt of your pair.
4. Step onto the cans, pull up on the rope loops with your hands, and start walking!
5. Make additional pairs of stilts as desired, with more cans and cord. Have stilt races with your friends.

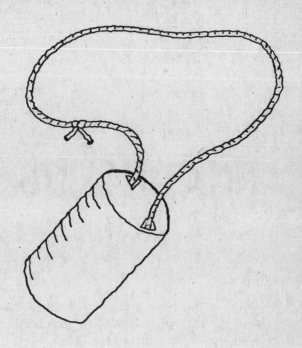

TIN CAN STARGAZING

Have fun looking at the stars in your own improvised planetarium—this makes a super science project!

You will need:

1. A large can with one end removed. (A 2-pound coffee can or large juice will do.)
2. Tracing paper and a pencil or a marking pen.
3. An ice pick or a hammer and a small nail.
4. A flashlight.

What to do:

1. Trace a circle on the paper, using your can as a pattern.
2. Copy a small picture in the circle of one of the constellations—the Big Dipper, the Seven Sisters, or whatever you wish.
3. Cut out the circle and tape on the closed end of the can.
4. Punch holes in the can through the tracing paper in the form of the constellation. Make small, neat holes. Remove the paper.
5. Put the flashlight into the opened end of the can. Turn out the lights in the room, and turn on the flashlight, aiming it at the ceiling. You will see the constellation large and bright on the ceiling.
6. Repeat with additional tin cans and other constellations.

TIN CAN LANTERNS

**You'll be fascinated by the flicker of candlelight
through your pierced-hole designs.**

You will need:

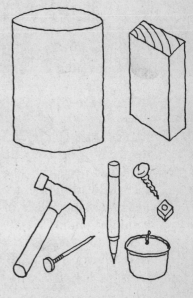

1. A tin can, any size, with one end removed.
2. A felt-tip marking pen.
3. A piece of wood, about as wide across as the can and short enough to handle easily.
4. A small hammer and a large nail.
5. A 1-inch screw and a nut that fits it.
6. A fat candle stub.
7. (Optional) a piece of picture-hanging wire.

10

What to do:

1. Wash the labels and glue from the can.
2. With the pen, draw a design onto the sides of the can. Note that the open end of the can is the top. (If you wish, work out your design first on a piece of paper and then copy it.)
3. Insert the wood into the can to keep it from bending in when you punch holes.

4. With the hammer and nail, punch holes along the design on the outside of the can.
5. Hammer the screw through the bottom of the can at the center so that the screw sticks up through the inside. Secure the screw with the nut.
6. Working carefully, push the candle down over the screw with a firm, rotating motion.
7. Light the candle and watch it flicker through your design.
8. If you like, punch holes near the top of the lantern on opposite sides. Twist a wire through with a big loop on top and hang your lantern.

TIN CAN MUSIC

**Want to make music, but have nothing to play?
Here's a quickie instrument
to make and pluck for fun.**

You will need:

1. An ice pick or a hammer and nail for punching 2 small holes in the can.
2. A large can, like a 2-pound coffee can.
3. A metal rasp or file.
4. Thin picture wire or nylon string. You'll see which works best for you.

You could also use rubber bands cut and tied together in a string.

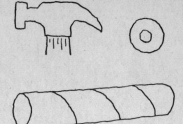

5. A metal washer, from a hardware store.
6. A cardboard tube from paper toweling.

What to do:

1. Punch a small hole in the center of the bottom of the can. Punch another hole near the top, on the side of the can. Smooth the edges with a rasp or file to keep rough edges from cutting the string.
2. Wrap and fasten one end of the wire or string tightly around the washer.

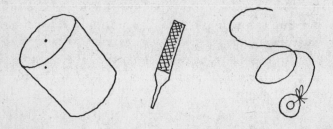

3. Thread the other end through the bottom hole from the inside of the can. Bring the string up the outside and thread it through the side hole to the inside of the can.
4. Make a small hole in the cardboard tube about 1 inch from the top. Thread the free end of the string through from the outside to the inside—over the top of the tube and into the hole and out again.

5. Place the bottom of the tube on the edge of the can and pull the wire so that there's no sag. (Lay both the can and the tube on a flat surface, in position, to do this.) You can loop the string over the top of the tube and out through the hole a few times. Tie a knot when it's tight.

6. Pick up the instrument and hold the tube up straight to make the string even tighter. Now you can pluck it to make music.

Food and Kitchen Things

HOW TO MAKE CLAY FROM BREAD

Which is more fun, making the clay or modeling with it? Mix this up and see!

You will need:

1. Six slices of white bread.
2. One teaspoon white household glue.
3. One-half teaspoon of liquid detergent.
4. A large mixing bowl and mixing spoon.
5. (Optional) food coloring or paint (tempera or acrylic).
6. (Optional) shellac and a brush to apply a protective coating.

What to do:

1. Cut the crusts off the bread.
2. Crumble the bread, letting the crumbs fall into the bowl.
3. Add the glue.
4. Add the detergent.
5. Stir together until well blended.
6. Knead the mixture with your hands. It will be sticky at first. Keep kneading. When you can form it into a ball and it no longer sticks, it is ready to use.
7. If the bread clay seems too sticky, add more bread crumbs. If too dry, add more glue.

How to use bread clay for modeling:

1. You can mix food coloring into the clay at step 4 above. Or paint the clay after your model is dry.
2. When you attach pieces (like a tail, for example), always glue them, even if they seem to stick by themselves. After the dough dries, pieces won't stick together without added glue.
3. See below for directions for making a pussycat from bread clay—and then you're on your own!
4. Store leftover bread dough in plastic bags to keep the dough moist until you use it next time.
5. After your completed model has dried thoroughly, you can brush on a coat of shellac to give it a glaze and keep it clean.

BREAD CLAY PUSSYCAT

**No one will believe you when you say
you made your cat from a few slices of bread!**

You will need:

1. A 2-inch ball of bread dough (directions, page 17).
2. A rolling pin and waxed paper.
3. White household glue.
4. A pen or pencil.
5. Rhinestones, beads, fancy buttons, or sequins from discarded jewelry and clothing.
6. (Optional) toothpicks.

What to do:

1. Roll the dough between 2 sheets of waxed paper into an egg-shaped pancake less than ½ inch thick at the narrower end, which is the top of the pancake.
2. Lift off the top sheet of paper. Shape the upper third of the pancake into a round partial-circle; this is the head.
3. Pinch out little triangles at the top of the head for ears.

4. Push in slightly under the head to shape the neck.
5. Push the dough down and out so that the cat will have a wide bottom. This part should be a little over ½ inch thick, so that the finished sculpture will be thicker at the bottom. Pick up the cat and try to sit it up by flattening the bottom surface against your work surface.
6. Twist out some dough from the cat's bottom to form a tail. Or roll out a separate piece of dough for the tail and attach it with glue.

7. Gently push the sides of the cat around toward the back to give it a rounded look.

8. Use the top of a pen or pencil to indent the eyes. Glue rhinestones or other decorative objects in as eyes.

9. For the mouth, make small indentations. For whiskers, roll out 6 very skinny strips of dough. Glue them above the mouth. Or use short pieces of toothpicks for whiskers.

10. Glue beads, sequins, or rhinestones around the neck for a collar.

11. If you haven't used colored dough, you can paint the cat as you wish.

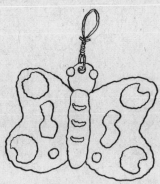

12. Hints for future projects: Make a variety of animals following the basic directions for the pussycat. If you make a tiny hole at the top of the head of each animal before the dough dries, you can put string or wire through the hole. With this hanger, build a mobile or decorate the Christmas tree.

DRIED KITCHEN STUFF PICTURE

Pasta and spice and everything nice—that's what this picture is made of!

You will need:

1. A few sheets of paper and a felt-tip marking pen.
2. White household glue.
3. A piece of wood or stiff cardboard, perhaps a side cut from a carton. The size could be about 12x16 inches.
4. Any dried foods in the kitchen. Look for interesting textures and colors. These are some possibilities:

Dried beans, all kinds   Tea leaves
Coffee beans and   Unpopped popcorn
  grinds   Barley
Rice   Tapioca
Salt   Seeds (poppy, celery,
Macaroni, all shapes   sesame, caraway)
Dried herbs (oregano,   Powdered spices (garlic,
  mint, basil, rosemary,   curry, paprika, chili,
  bay leaf)   mustard)

5. (Optional) tempera or acrylic paints.

What to do:

1. Draw a design or picture on paper to use as a guide when you make your picture.
2. On the wood or cardboard, fill in a small section of the design or picture at a time. First cover the area with a thick layer of glue. Place on the glue the beans, macaroni, seeds, or whatever you've decided on, until this part of the design or picture is covered up.
3. Fill in the spaces between the larger beans and other materials with finer material, such as powdered spices. Sprinkle it well over the glued spot, beans and all.
4. Keep gluing and filling small areas of the design this way until the entire design is glued and covered.
5. The background or uncovered area behind the design can be filled in by one of two ways. Spread glue on the background and dust powdered spices over it. Or paint it with tempera or acrylic paints.

LEAF-DECORATED EGGS

Too beautiful to eat!

You will need:

1. Tiny flowers, leaves, blades of grass.
2. Salad oil.
3. Hard-cooked white eggs, boiled in the shell.

4. Old nylon stockings.
5. String or small rubber bands.
6. Egg dyes or vegetable food coloring.
7. Vinegar.
8. Teacups, mugs, or small bowls for a color bath.
9. A wire cookie rack for drying eggs.

What to do:

1. Wash the flowers, leaves, and grasses gently in water to remove any dust. Dry them between layers of newspaper or paper towels.
2. Dip the flowers and leaves into a bit of salad oil. Pat off any excess oil with a paper towel.
3. Arrange the leaves on the eggshell.
4. Slip a 6-inch section of stocking over the egg. Tie the end snugly but not too tightly around the egg with string or rubber bands.
5. Prepare the dye or food coloring as directed, with a bit of vinegar.
6. Dip the stocking-wrapped egg into the color bath until the egg turns the shade you want.
7. Remove the wrapping and leaves, and dry the egg on a wire rack.

POTATO PRINTING

Gutenberg did very well in his way, but your own potato printing is a lot more fun.

You will need:

1. A potato (a carrot, radish, apple, or a cork can substitute).
2. A knife.
3. Poster paint and brushes.
4. Scrap paper and paper for printing.

What to do:

1. Cut the potato into quarters or thick slices. The pieces are your printing blocks.
2. Carve the surface of each block as carefully as possible in a simple design. Nicks, cuts, gouges, and scallops create interesting designs. Or use a whole uncarved piece that has its own interesting shape.
3. Try out the shapes on scrap paper. First paint the carved surface and press it down evenly on the paper. Don't wiggle or twist as you press, or the paint will smear and make a blurred shape.
4. Experiment to see how much paint prints best for you. When you find the design and the amount of paint are right, begin printing on your good paper.
5. Use different colors and shapes. Fit several printing units together to form larger designs.
6. To change color, wash the piece of potato off, dry it with a paper towel, and paint it with another color.

MAKE YOUR OWN FINGER PAINTS

**Why go out and buy paints in a toy shop?
It's more fun to mix up your own!**

You will need:

1. Three-fourths cup of cornstarch.
2. A saucepan, small bowl or cup, and mixing spoon.
3. One envelope of unflavored gelatin.
4. One-half cup of detergent or soap flakes.

5. Four small jars with lids.
6. Liquid food coloring (vegetable dye).
7. Glazed shelf paper, from a variety store or supermarket.

What to do:

1. Mix the cornstarch and ¾ cup of cold water in a saucepan. If you have a wire whisk, that will be helpful.
2. Empty the gelatin into a small bowl containing ¼ cup of cold water. Let stand.
3. Returning to the cornstarch mixture, stir 2 cups of hot water into it. Stir as you cook over low heat until the mixture is smooth and begins to boil.
4. Remove the saucepan carefully from the stove to your work space. Add the gelatin–cold water mixture and blend it in.
5. Add the detergent or soap flakes. Stir until fully dissolved. This makes about 3 cups of finger painting base.
6. Put equal portions of the mixture into the 4 jars.
7. Add about 1 teaspoon of dye to each jar, one color to a jar—red, yellow, green, and blue. Stir to blend in the color.
8. The paints are now ready! Cover a table with thick sections of newspaper, tear off a piece of the shelf paper, dampen the paper with a moist sponge or rag, and start painting.
9. Don't forget to wash your fingers when you change colors so the colors won't get muddied.

SUGAR-CUBE COLLAGE

If someone asks you what kind of art this is, smile
knowingly and say, "Cubism, of course."

You will need:

1. Sugar cubes.
2. Poster paints in jars and a pan or tray to hold them.
3. Paintbrushes.
4. Very stiff cardboard (a side cut from a carton box, for example) or wood, about 9x12 inches.
5. White household glue.
6. A stick-on picture hook.

What to do:

1. Spread out the sugar cubes.
2. Set out the paints in your tray or pan, and put a brush with each color. If you have more colors than brushes, dip the brushes in a container of water and dry on a rag or paper towel to avoid muddying the colors.
3. Paint the sides of each cube while holding the top and bottom between your thumb and index finger. Set it down to paint the top. The bottom is left unpainted. Use different colors for the sides and tops.
4. Let the cubes dry completely before the next step.

5. Start in the center of the wood or cardboard and begin gluing on your painted cubes, working out toward the edges. Use enough glue; cover the bottom of each cube completely.

6. Create an interesting design with the cubes. Make a swirl effect or a geometric design. Mix up the colors. Leave a border of cardboard or wood about 1 inch or so all around. You may want to have a straight edge of cubes just inside the border, and paint the border with one of your cube colors.

7. Let the finished collage dry overnight. Attach the stick-on hook and hang it proudly on the wall!

HOW TO MAKE PLAY DOUGH

Kitchen magic turns two cheap ingredients, plus water, into great modeling material.

You will need:

1. A saucepan and stirring spoon or wire whisk.
2. Four cups of baking soda.
3. Two cups of cornstarch.
4. Two and one-half cups of water.
5. Aluminum foil.
6. A damp cloth and a plastic bag.
7. (Optional) poster paints, shellac, and paintbrushes.

What to do:

1. In a saucepan, mix the baking soda, cornstarch, and water. Blend thoroughly. A wire whisk will be a help.
2. Stir with a spoon over medium heat until the mixture gets doughy. Scoop it out onto a sheet of aluminum foil and let it cool until it's comfortable to handle.
3. Knead the mixture until it's fairly smooth—about 2 to 3 minutes.
4. Wrap in a damp cloth and store in a plastic bag until you're ready to model with it.

Modeling tips:

1. You can make the same things with this clay as with any other modeling clay. However, big pieces of play dough may crack while drying. With experience, you'll see how big a piece to model.
2. It takes about 2 or 3 days or more for the play dough to dry, depending on the size of the piece and the humidity. Drying can be speeded up in an oven at its lowest setting; again, since ovens and sizes of sculpture will vary, you will have to let experience tell you how long this will take.
3. After your pieces have dried, you can paint them with poster paints. After the paint dries, brush on shellac for a shiny protective coating.

Things to Do When You Go Someplace Where There Are No Kids to Play With

Flip Card Movies

Parachute Kite

Fingerprint Designs

FLIP CARD MOVIES

**No need to be bored when you can
create your own action.**

You will need:

1. A stack of 3x5-inch cards, or a small
   notebook with about 25 pages.
2. A pen or pencil.

What to do:

1. For your first movie, make something simple, like the
   stick figure of a man.
2. Draw the figure on the last page of your book or the
   bottom card of the stack.
3. Leave about a 1-inch space at the top of each picture
   where you'll be holding the notebook or stack of
   cards.
4. On the second page or card, draw almost the ,ame
   picture, but change the placement of an arm or leg
   very slightly.

5. Continue with additional drawings, with at least 20 or 25 in the sequence. Move the arm or leg up or down, or change the legs slightly each time to show the figure walking or running.

6. After finishing the drawings, arrange the cards or notebook with the first drawing on the bottom. Holding the stack or notebook at the top with one hand, use the thumb and index finger of the other to flip through the pictures so that the cards or pages fall down one after the other.

7. Flip with a smooth motion. See what flipping faster and slower does to the action. See how your figure appears to move, like a movie cartoon.

8. Next time, try a more complicated and longer movie.

PARACHUTE KITE

Fly it indoors anytime—outdoors, too, when the wind isn't too strong. A puff of breath is enough.

You will need:

1. Tissues (the nose-blowing kind).
2. A spool of fine thread.
3. A ballast or weight (for example, an ice-cream stick, a washer, a small piece of heavy cardboard, or a wad of crumpled-up newspaper).
4. (Optional) cellophane tape.

What to do:

1. Separate the 2 layers of a tissue carefully and discard one. You will now have a very lightweight piece of paper.
2. Cut 4 pieces of thread 10 inches long, and 1 piece 15 inches long.
3. Tie a piece of 10-inch thread to each corner of the tissue. Do this very carefully to avoid rips.
4. Tie the loose ends of the 4 threads together in a knot.
5. To this knot, tie an end of the longer thread. To the other end of the thread, attach your weight by tying or taping.
6. Fly by tossing the weight and parachute into the air, or suspend it from as high as you can reach and let it float down.
7. Variation: Discard the 15-inch piece of thread. Instead of that piece, at step 5 attach the end of the thread on the spool. See if you can blow the parachute kite upward and keep it in the air. A very gentle breeze or your own breath can keep it aloft.

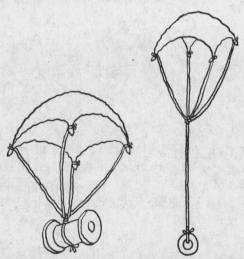

FINGERPRINT DESIGNS

If you go to a place
where there are no kids to play with,
grab that ink pad to take along with you.

What you need:

1. Your fingers.
2. An ink pad.
3. Paper.
4. Felt-tip pens.

What to do:

1. To get your imagination going, look at the pictures showing how fingerprints have been made into all kinds of designs.
2. Gently press your fingertips on an ink pad and then onto paper.

3. Fill up the paper with as many or as few fingerprints as you wish. Clump them in flowerlike petals, or cats sitting on a fence, or anything else that takes your fancy.

4. Decorate the design by outlining with the pen. You may want to use more than one color.

5. You can combine several fingerprints into pretty designs.

Gift Things

Design a Shirt

Postage-Stamp Locket

Decoupage Stone Paperweight

Decoupage Soda-Bottle Vase

Crayon Batik Shirt

Woven Place Mats

Potpourri Jars

Soap on a Rope

DESIGN A SHIRT

**What friend wouldn't be happy
with a personalized T-shirt you've made?**

You will need:

1. Wax crayons.
2. Scrap paper.
3. A T-shirt.
4. A damp cloth.
5. An iron.
6. (Optional) a black felt-tip waterproof
   pen or India ink and a brush.

What to do:

1. Make up a design with crayons on scrap paper. A huge
   initial might be fun, or perhaps a T for T-shirt.
2. Copy your design on the shirt with crayon. Fill it in
   with crayons in assorted colors.
3. Put the T-shirt on the ironing board and cover with
   the damp cloth. Press with a hot iron to fix the design.
4. When the T-shirt is cool to the touch, you can outline or embellish the design with the black pen or
   India ink.

41

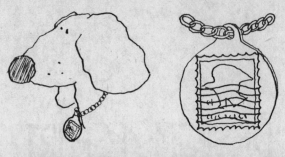

POSTAGE-STAMP LOCKET

There's great art on stamps, and the cancellation marks add that certain something!

You will need:

1. A canceled postage stamp. Pick a handsome one.
2. An old dog-license tag. Beg or salvage an out-of-date tag.
3. White household glue.
4. Clear plastic spray, from a hobby or art supply shop.
5. Gold paint and a small brush.
6. A "gold" jewelry chain, small enough to go through the hole in the dog tag, from a variety store or hobby shop.

What to do:

1. Tear the stamped corner off an envelope. Soak in water for a few minutes to remove the stamp without tearing it. Let the stamp dry.
2. Trim the stamp, if necessary, to fit on the dog tag. Do not cover the hole of the tag.
3. Apply glue to the back of the stamp and press it onto the tag. Do not cover the hole.
4. When thoroughly dry, after an hour or so, spray the stamp.
5. When the spray has dried, paint around the stamp to cover the metal left showing.
6. Slip the locket onto the chain.

DECOUPAGE STONE PAPERWEIGHT

**When a stone gets this gussied up,
it's fit to be a paperweight.**

You will need:

1. A large stone or rock, about 3 to 4 inches across. Look for a smooth, flat one.
2. A small, colorful picture cut from an old magazine.
3. Scissors.
4. White household glue.
5. Clear shellac and a small brush.

What to do:

1. Scrub the stone with soap and water. Rinse and dry it thoroughly.
2. Study the stone to see how it lies best, and decide which surface is the top you will decorate.
3. Cut out the picture.
4. Apply glue to the back of the picture and place it on the rock, making sure to press the picture into any crevices or hollows in the rock. If you use enough glue to soak the picture, it will be fairly flexible.
5. When the glue is dry, brush on the shellac and let it dry again.

* *Decoupage* comes from the French word *découper,* which means to cut out. It is the art of decorating by applying cut-out pictures to an object and then coating the surface with several layers of finish.

DECOUPAGE SODA-BOTTLE VASE

If you use a no-return bottle, don't forget to write on the gift tag, "Many happy returns!"

You will need:

1. A small-size soda bottle.

2. Acrylic or latex paint, any color you like, and a paintbrush.
3. Designs or pictures from magazines, greeting cards, or catalogues.
4. Scissors.
5. White household glue.
6. Shellac and a brush.

What to do:

1. Rinse and dry the soda bottle.
2. Brush on the paint to cover the entire bottle. Let it dry.
3. While the paint is drying, select and cut out pictures and designs. Arrange them in scenes or designs to go up and down or spiral around the bottle.
4. Glue the pictures onto the bottle.
5. Let the glue dry.
6. Brush on the shellac and let it dry.

CRAYON BATIK SHIRT

Melted crayon bits (handle with care) are the fascinating ingredient for a super-special gift.

You will need:

1. Colored crayons.
2. A muffin tin.
3. A white T-shirt.
4. A soft pencil.
5. A pot holder.
6. Q-Tips.
7. An iron.
8. Waxed paper.

What to do:

1. Put bits of crayon, one color to a cup, into the muffin tin.
2. Set the oven at 175° to 200°. Let the muffin tin warm until the crayons melt. *Watch it carefully.*
3. While the crayons are melting, draw a design on the T-shirt with the pencil.
4. Remove the tin with the melted crayons from the oven, being sure to handle it carefully with a pot holder. Set it near you on a rack or trivet.
5. Dip a Q-Tip into some melted crayon. Paint on the design little by little, working fast so that the crayon won't solidify on the Q-Tip.
6. Set the iron to warm, not hot.

7. Place the waxed paper over the design and iron over the paper to set the colors.

WOVEN PLACE MATS

A set of place mats for your favorite homemaker is a thoughtful gift.

You will need:

1. Corrugated cardboard, about 14 inches square, from the side of a carton.
2. A large plate or pot lid, about 12 inches in diameter, to use as a pattern, and a pencil to trace around it.
3. A large nail.
4. A large, blunt needle with a big eye.
5. White cotton string.
6. An assortment of odd lengths and various colors of heavy yarn.
7. Small scissors with points, like manicure scissors.
8. A damp cloth and an iron.

What to do:

1. Draw a circle on the cardboard, tracing around your pattern with the pencil.
2. Mark dots around the circle, about ½ inch apart. Make sure to have an odd number of dots.
3. With the nail, punch holes through the cardboard on the dots.

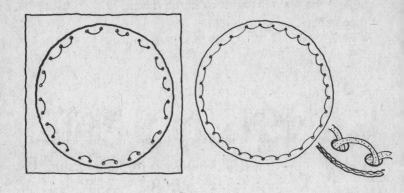

4. Thread the needle with a piece of string. The string should be a little more than twice the length around the circle. Allow about 12 inches extra.

5. Sew in and out through the holes around the circle. The first time around, the stitches will alternate, a stitch on top of the cardboard and a loop beneath. Go around again, filling in the blanks so that you have stitches of string on top connecting all the holes.

6. Thread the needle with a piece of yarn about 4 feet long.

7. Slip the needle over and under one string stitch a couple of times to anchor it, leaving an end a few

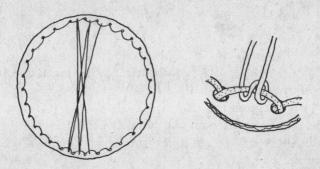

inches long. Draw the yarn across the circle at the center and onto the opposite point of the circle. Slip the needle over and under the string stitch there to anchor the yarn.

8. Now go clockwise to the next string stitch and anchor the yarn the same way. Draw the yarn again across the circle, passing the center point, over to the other side. Anchor the yarn to the string stitch, which will be next to the stitch you started with. Go clockwise to the next stitch and anchor the yarn again.

9. Repeat steps 7 and 8 until you have gone all around the circle, crossing the center each time you go from one side to the other. Tie loose ends of the yarn to each other as needed when the yarn runs out. You will now have the circle filled in with spokes of yarn. These are your warps for weaving.

10. Your weaving wefts will be yarn woven in and out, above and under the warps. Thread a piece of yarn, any length, into your needle.

11. Loop the end of the piece of yarn around some of the warps at the center or hub of the circle and knot loosely. Start weaving with the needle around the knot. Weave outward, making bigger and bigger circles around the starting point.

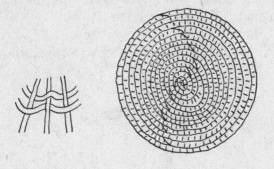

12. Weave to the end of the piece of yarn and slip off the needle. Rethread with another piece of yarn. Start the new thread 3 or 4 warps back from where the last piece of yarn ran out, overlapping the weaving to hold the loose ends. Choose matching and contrasting colors of yarn to make an interesting pattern. As you weave, pull the yarn gently so that it is barely snug, neither tight nor loose.

13. Continue the weaving until the circle is filled with woven yarn.

14. Finish off by threading a length of yarn around the outside, catching all the end loops of the warps. Don't overlook any of the end loops. Knot loose ends and work them into the woven mat with the needle.

15. With the scissors, snip through the string loops that have held the warp loops in place. Careful! Don't cut into the yarn! Lift the finished place mat off the cardboard.

16. With the iron set at medium heat, cover the mat with the damp cloth and press it flat.

17. For additional place mats, you can use the same cardboard and start over, sewing string through the holes.

9. Whenever a delightful scent is wanted, remove the lid and let the fragrance fill the room.

(See also "Sachets" in *Thread and Needle Things* for another sweet-smelling idea.)

SOAP ON A ROPE

Anyone who has ever dropped the soap in the shower will love you for this one!

You will need:

1. Bits and pieces of leftover soap.
2. A double boiler.
3. A spoon or wooden stick.
4. (Optional) vegetable coloring.
5. A pot holder.
6. A muffin tin or small juice cans.
7. Rope in 24-inch pieces.

What to do:

1. Put the pieces of soap into the top pan of the double boiler. Various colors of soap can be used.
2. Put an inch or so of water into the bottom pan of the double boiler.
3. Set the top pan into the bottom pan, and put on a stove burner. Turn to medium heat.
4. When the water boils, lower the heat and stir the soap with the spoon or stick. Add vegetable coloring if desired. Keep stirring until the soap has melted.

5. Turn off the burner and remove the top pan carefully, using the pot holder.

6. Carefully pour the melted soap into muffin tins or juice cans.

7. When the soap begins to cool and congeal, loop a piece of rope and put both ends into the soap, one piece to each container of soap. Let the soap continue to harden.

8. When the soap is completely hard, run hot water over the bottom and sides of the muffin tin or cans, or dip into hot water, to loosen soap. It will slip out of the form all ready for you to wrap as a gift.

Thread-and-Needle Things

Sew a Burlap Bag

Make a Bib Apron

Glove Finger Puppets

Sachets

A Felt "Pillow" Pillow

Sock Animal Puppet

SEW A BURLAP BAG

**Make a burly burlap bag you'll love forever.
(It's a good gift idea, too!)**

You will need:

1. A piece of burlap, about 20x30 inches.
2. A soft pencil.
3. A needle, straight pins, and heavy-duty thread.
4. Acrylic paints and a small brush for each color.
5. Sewing scissors.
6. Six lengths of yarn, each about 28 inches long.
7. A large needle with a very large eye.

What to do:

1. Fold the burlap in half lengthwise. Pin the 2 long edges together.
2. Measure 6 inches up from the bottom along the pinned edge. Mark this point with the pencil.
3. Sew a seam from the top down along the pinned edge, about ¾ inch in from the edge, to the pencil mark, and sew back up to the top. Double stitching is needed on the loosely woven burlap. Sew small stitches.

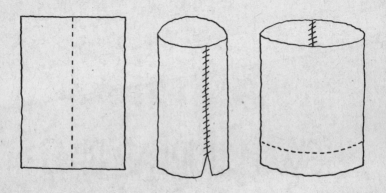

4. Lay the burlap tube on your work surface and push it around to make the seam run up the center back instead of the side. Flatten smooth with your fingers.
5. Pin the bottom edges together. Sew a seam across it 6 inches up from the bottom edge.
6. Paint a decorative design on the front of the bag. Let the paint dry completely before going on to the next step.
7. Begin pulling out crosswise burlap threads from the bottom edge. Pull gently at the bottom thread. Work one thread at a time. You will see a fringe beginning

to form. If needed, you can snip a crosswise thread to release it; be sure not to cut a fringe (lengthwise) thread. Continue making the fringe until you get ½ inch or so from the bag's bottom seam.

8. Hold your lengths of yarn together so that the ends are even. Knot one end together.

9. Pin the knot to something firm (a pillow, for example) or put a heavy paperweight on it to hold it. Separate the threads into 3 strands of 2 threads each. Braid the 3 strands to the end, and hold the end between your fingers.

10. Thread the unknotted end of braid through the large needle. Working about 1 inch from the top of the bag, and starting from the center front, sew around the bag in large stitches, about ½ to ¾ inch long. You will end up a stitch-length away from where you started.

11. Pull the needle off the braid drawstring. Rebraid the loose end, if necessary, and knot it. Now you can pull on the drawstring to close the bag.

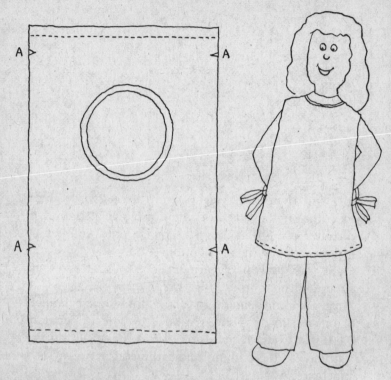

MAKE A BIB APRON

**This is a classic you'll want to wear
even when there's no barbecue.
Looks great over jeans!**

You will need:

1. Blue-and-white-striped ticking, cut to 16 inches in width and about 48 inches in length (longer for a 6-footer, shorter for someone under 5 feet tall).

2. A plate 8 inches in diameter to use as a pattern.
3. A felt-tip pen or soft pencil.
4. Sewing scissors.
5. Straight pins, a needle, and bright red or orange thread.
6. About 2½ yards of seam binding, the same color as the thread.

What to do:

1. Lay the material out flat. Using the plate as a pattern, trace around it on the fabric with the pen or pencil. To place the circle: Mark a point in the center of the ticking, measuring from side to side, and ⅓ of the length down from the top edge of the fabric. Center the plate on this point.
2. Cut out the circle.
3. Lay the fabric out flat and pin up 1-inch hems at the top and bottom edges. Sew the hems.
4. Working from the wrong side (inner side) of the fabric, pin the seam binding around the neck edge. Half the width of the binding should stick out beyond the neck edge. Cut off the excess length and sew. Remove the pins.
5. Working on the right side of the material, fold the loose edge of the seam binding over the fabric and pin down, covering the raw edge of the fabric. Sew around the neck.
6. Try on the apron. Mark at the points shown (A in the drawing) to indicate your waistline.
7. Cut four 10-inch pieces of seam binding for ties. Sew an end of each tie to one of the 4 marked points of the apron.
8. Put on the apron and tie it at the waist.

GLOVE
FINGER PUPPETS

**They're fun to make—and let your fingers
do the talking!**

You will need:

1. One lone fabric glove (every house has one!).
2. Sewing scissors.
3. Needle and thread.
4. Felt-tip pens in assorted colors.
5. White household glue.
6. Scraps of yarn, sequins, fringe, felt, small buttons, and other colorful little things.

What to do:

1. Cut the fingers from the glove. Cut close to the palm.
2. Sew tiny overcasting stitches around the cut ends of the glove fingers to prevent raveling. Don't sew the

opening closed; sew one thickness of fabric.

3. With the felt-tip pens, draw on funny faces, people, animals, flowers, as you wish. Make a family, or a group of kids, or a menagerie.

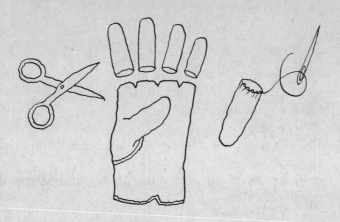

4. Glue on sequins, pieces of felt, and the like to make eyes, mouth, ears, hair, and whatever.
5. Put on a puppet show, or have your friends "finger" their own puppets.

SACHETS

**Mm, mm, smells good. An old-fashioned idea
whose time has come—again.**

You will need:

1. Petals from fragrant flowers, such as lilac, rose, honey-suckle, or others blooming in your yard.
2. Shallow pans for drying.
3. Paper towels.
4. Calico fabric, cut into two 3-inch squares for each sachet.
5. Sewing scissors, straight pins, needle, and thread to match the calico.

What to do:

1. A week or so before making the sachets, lay your gathered flower petals loosely in pans that you have lined with paper towels. Let them stand in a cool, dry place away from light. A closet shelf will do.
2. When the week is up, crunch the petals into tiny flakes.
3. Lay the brightly colored sides of 2 squares of calico face-to-face. Line up the edges and pin them together.
4. Stitch around 3 sides and turn the square inside out so that the seams are now inside.
5. Fill the calico sack with crushed flower petals.
6. Pin the open ends together, raw edges inside, and sew with tiny stitches that scarcely show.
7. Put the finished sachets in closets or clothing drawers to make things smell fresh and flowery.

A FELT
"PILLOW" PILLOW

**In case your friends don't know what a pillow is,
you can label this one.**

You will need:

1. A large brown paper bag, cut to open up and lie flat.
2. A felt-tip marking pen and a pencil.
3. Scissors.
4. A piece of felt about the same size in a contrasting color.
5. Two pieces of felt about 15 inches square, or 3 inches bigger in both directions than your pillow. Buy the felt at a hobby or fabric shop.

6. White household glue.
7. Straight pins, a needle, and thread to match the felt squares.
8. A 12x12-inch foam pillow, 2 inches thick, or a similar size pillow sold at a variety store.

What to do:

1. On the brown paper bag, draw with your pencil a square the size of the pillow. Draw inside it, in as large letters as possible, the word "PILLOW" in capital letters. The letters must be thick so that you can

cut them out. Make them ¼-inch thick at all points.

2. Cut out the letters. Set them on the contrasting felt piece, and trace around them with the marking pen.

3. Cut out the felt letters carefully.

4. Lay one of the felt squares on your working surface. Arrange the letters as you like on the square. Allow space for at least a 2-inch border all around, so that the letters won't run over onto the sides of the finished pillow.

5. Pick up one letter at a time, apply glue generously to the underside, and stick it back on the felt square. Press gently but firmly to make a good bond. When all the letters are glued in place, set aside to dry thoroughly, several hours or overnight.

6. Sew the decorated pillow top to the other square of felt. Pin together on 3 sides, then stitch around about ½ inch in from the edges of the felt.

7. Insert the foam pillow into the felt case. Pin the open side together and continue sewing around the pillow.

SOCK ANIMAL PUPPET

Got imagination-plus?
Start with a big lollygagging red tongue
and go on from there!

You will need:

1. A darning egg or lightbulb. (Handle gently.)
2. A knee sock missing its mate.
3. Two small buttons.

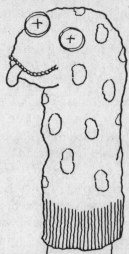

4. Red embroidery thread.
5. Scissors.
6. A scrap of red felt.
7. A needle and thread.
8. An assortment of scraps: yarn, felt, cloth, and ribbon.

What to do:

1. Insert the darning egg or lightbulb into the sock so that you will avoid sewing the sock to itself.
2. Sew buttons on as eyes, about 2 inches up from the toe, depending on the size of the sock.
3. Embroider a mouth with the red thread.
4. Get a U-shaped piece of red felt. Sew the straight end to the mouth to make the hanging-out tongue.
5. Make ears from felt scraps: for an elephant, big, round ears (and matching trunk); for a hound, long, floppy ears; for a cat, triangular ears that stand up. Use your imagination.
6. Trim with ribbon bows and collars, yarn manes—anything you fancy.

68

Outdoor Things

Sand Casting at the Beach

Bird Feeder

Skatemobile

SAND CASTING AT THE BEACH

Can't get enough of the beach? Bring home this impressive souvenir you made yourself.

You will need:

1. A fine sunny day, a beach, and at least 4 hours to spend there.
2. Four pieces of wood or corrugated cardboard. You might find pieces of driftwood.
3. Shells, smooth beach glass, pebbles, driftwood fragments, and any small beachcombing treasures, but nothing organic that would rot.
4. Two or 3 pounds of white plaster of Paris, bought at a hardware store.
5. A pail and spoon for mixing.
6. Another pail for water.
7. A wire loop for hanging, which you can make ahead of time from a piece of coat hanger.

What to do:

1. Arrange the wood or cardboard in the sand to make a frame. Stand on edge and prop with sand hills outside the frame. The space inside will be the size of your casting. Keep it small, about 12 inches square or so. You want to be able to carry it home!

2. Smooth the sand inside the frame. Add your beach things, face down, arranged in a pleasing pattern. Remember, what's face down will be facing out of the casting later. Also draw patterns in the smooth sand with a stick or your finger.

3. Pour about half or more of the plaster of Paris into the mixing pail. Add enough water to make it the consistency of heavy cream, stir, and pour immediately into your frame. The plaster hardens fast and suddenly.

4. The casting should be at least 1½ inches thick. If you need to add more, mix it up right away and pour it into the frame.

5. Before the plaster of Paris starts to harden, stick the ends of the wire loop into the casting near what will be the top end. Hold or support the loop in place until the plaster hardens.

6. Let the casting bake in the sun for 4 hours while you entertain yourself in other ways. Test the plaster with your finger for dampness. It may require more baking. It must be fully dry before you move it.

7. Remove the casting frame and lift up your casting. Brush and blow away excess sand. Your sand casting is ready to hang on your wall as soon as you get home.

BIRD FEEDER

**Birds of a feather flock together—to your house!
Make this easy feeding station.**

You will need:

1. Scissors.
2. A ½-gallon milk carton.
3. White household glue.
4. A piece of lightweight wood cut in a square 2 inches wider and longer than the carton.

5. A piece of plastic fishing line or thin wire.
6. A tree to hang the feeder on.
7. Wild bird seed.

What to do:

1. With the point of the scissors, poke a small hole in one side of the carton, about 3 inches from the bottom.

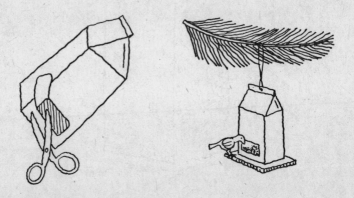

2. Cutting out from the hole, cut up and around to make an opening for the birds to stick their heads through for feeding. The hole will be about 3 inches high and narrower than the width of the carton (don't cut out to the corners). The bottom of the hole should be 2 inches up from the bottom of the carton.
3. Glue the piece of wood onto the bottom of the carton, so that it sticks out 1 inch on all sides.
4. Poke a small hole in the center top of the carton.
5. Cut a piece of line or wire. The length depends on the height of your tree branch. Measure from the branch to the level you want the feeder to be, and add a few inches.

6. Thread an end of the line or wire through the hole in the top of the carton, and knot close to the carton.
7. Fill with bird seed.
8. Tie the other end of the line or wire to the tree branch.

SKATEMOBILE

**With a pair of skates, you and a friend
can have fun!
(Directions are for one skatemobile.)**

You will need:

1. An orange crate, from the supermarket or fruit store.
2. Two strips of wood 12 inches long, 2½ inches wide, and ½ inch thick.
3. A hammer.
4. About 2 dozen 2-inch nails (6-penny size).
5. A 30-inch-long piece of 2x4-inch lumber.
6. One roller skate and a skate key.

What to do:

1. Stand the crate on its narrow end, with the open side facing you. Nail the 2 strips of wood onto the top of the crate in a wide, inverted-V pattern. The point of the V will be at the far side of the crate, and the ends of the V will protrude about 6 inches over the sides of the crate to make the steering handles (see illustration). Nail the handles in place.

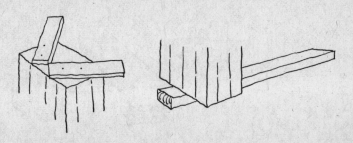

2. Set the 2x4 on the ground. Set the crate onto it, keeping the handle end as the top, and the point of the inverted-V as the front of the skatemobile. The front of the crate should be set back about 6 inches from the front end of the 2x4. Also, center the crate from side to side over the 2x4 so it will be balanced when you ride the skatemobile.

3. Nail the crate to the 2x4, using about 8 nails to make sure it's securely held together.
4. Take the skate apart by loosening the center (length-adjustment) screw.
5. Turn the skatemobile over and brace it so it stands firmly in the upside-down position.

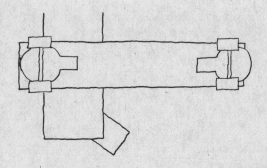

6. Place the heel end of the skate on the rear end of the 2x4 and nail it in place through the holes in the skate. Use enough nails to fasten it securely. If there is a heel plate in the way, place it so that it goes around the end of the 2x4.

7. Remove and discard the shoe clamps on the toe end of the skate. Attach the toe end of the skate to the front end of the 2x4 as described in step 6. Now your skate-mobile is finished—turn it over and give it a spin.

Art Things

Bleach Picture

Rubbing Design Picture

A Different Collage

Fish Print

Paper Mosaic

Window Shade Picture

Painting Old Shoes and Sneakers

Spatter Painting

Aluminum Foil Engraving

Wax-on-Canvas Painting

Scratch-Out Painting

Papier-mâché Balloon Mask

Soap Sculpture

BLEACH PICTURE

You get fantastic results painting
with ordinary old household bleach.
This is easy and different!

You will need:

1. Colored construction paper.
2. Bleach—ordinary household bleach.*
3. A discarded china cup or glass that will not be used later for drinking.
4. A paintbrush.
5. Felt-tip marking pens, black and colors.

* Wear an apron or old clothes.

What to do:

1. Lay a sheet of construction paper on your work surface.
2. Pour about 1/4 cup of bleach into the cup or glass. *Caution!* If you get bleach on your hands or elsewhere, wash off immediately and thoroughly.
3. Dip the brush into the bleach and start painting. Experiment to see what special effects you can get, and then paint a masterpiece on a fresh sheet of paper.
4. When the painting is completed, let it dry. Outline parts of the painting with marking pens to accentuate a design or fill in the background. Use black alone, or contrasting colors.

RUBBING DESIGN PICTURE

It's easy to get professional results
with rubbing! You'll amaze yourself
with your own beautiful work.

You will need:

1. Paper: plain white paper, rice paper, or any light-weight paper you have around. The size depends on the surface you'll be rubbing.
2. Surfaces to rub: Any slightly raised surface will do. For practice, start with coins. Look for crockery with raised designs, embossed trays, stone carvings, manhole covers, gravestones, tree leaves and tree bark, pressed flowers, and anything else with a three-dimensional effect.
3. Crayons or charcoal, from an art supply store.
4. Paint or ink, and a paintbrush.

What to do:

1. Place the paper on the surface of the object you are going to rub. Hold it in place with one hand, or you may wish to tape it. (Masking tape is good.)
2. With crayon or charcoal, rub evenly over the whole design.
3. You'll see that the higher parts of the design are darker. Practice pressing heavily and lightly to get

special effects. Experiment with different types of paper and different ways of holding the crayon and charcoal.

4. Outline the rubbings with paint or ink. Experiment with colors—black, gold, or others.
5. You can collect rubbings of one kind of thing you like especially. Keep your eyes peeled for interesting rubbing surfaces wherever you go!

A DIFFERENT COLLAGE

**The materials are unusual, but the results
are fit to be framed and hung.**

You will need:

1. White household glue.
2. A stretched canvas or a canvas board, from an art supply store. Or a stiff cardboard that you could cut from the side of a carton box.
3. Sand, from the beach, a sandbox, or a builders' supply store.
4. Gravel. Interesting colored gravel can be found in garden and aquarium stores.
5. Sawdust. (Save it when someone saws wood.)
6. Poster paints and brushes.

What to do:

1. Dribble and smear glue thickly in various shapes and sizes on the canvas or cardboard.

2. Dribble sand in one spot until the glue is thoroughly covered. Gently pat the sand into the glue with your fingers. In another area, gently press gravel into the glue. And in another, the sawdust.
3. Play around with colors and textures. Use any combination you like.
4. Let the collage dry. Gently brush and blow off the excess materials.
5. You may want to add more to the surface. Apply more glue and add the sand, sawdust, and gravel. Don't be timid.
6. The dried collage can be touched up with paint. A border painted in a coordinated color is a good finishing touch.

FISH PRINT

**Let others do the ordinary.
You can be the first in the neighborhood
to ink and print a flounder!**

You will need:

1. A fresh whole fish, preferably a flat one like a flounder. Someone who's been fishing might give you an extra fish, or you might surprise a fish store owner into giving you one when he learns what your plan is.
2. Paper towels.
3. India ink, black or colored, and a small paintbrush.
4. Several sheets of rice paper, from an art supply store.

5. (Optional) paints and brushes.
6. (Optional) picture frame with glass and wire for hanging.

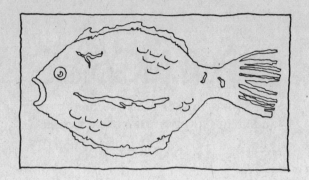

What to do:

1. Wash the fish and pat it dry with paper toweling. Let it stand for half an hour or so to make sure it's dry.
2. Lay the fish on your working surface and paint one entire side of the fish with India ink. Cover completely, but leave no blobs or pools of ink.
3. Carefully place the inked fish, inked side down, on a sheet of rice paper. Gently press the fish with your fingers so that all parts of it make contact with the paper. Avoid smudging by being sure not to make the fish slide on the paper.
4. Carefully lift off the fish. You will now see a print of the fish on the paper, scales and all.
5. Sometimes the first print is too inky. Try a second pressing on another piece of paper. Practice will show you the best way to ink the fish.
6. Let the print dry. If you wish, you can frame it just as it is.

7. Or, if you like, you can paint highlights on the print with colored inks or paints. Then dry again and consider framing it to hang on your wall.

PAPER MOSAIC

**Save your scraps of pretty colored paper
and create lovely symmetrical designs.**

You will need:

1. Several sheets of drawing paper.
2. Scissors.
3. White household glue or rubber cement.
4. A piece of cardboard.
5. A pencil or felt-tip marking pen.
6. Colored paper in varied colors, scraps or larger pieces.

What to do:

1. Fold a sheet of drawing paper in half.
2. Cut into the doubled sheet to make a fancy shape. Cut curved lines, straight lines, or zigzags, but don't cut too many lines.
3. Open up your paper. Does the shape remind you of anything? Is it pleasing to your eye? Take other sheets of paper and try other ways of cutting.
4. Look over your cutout designs and select your favorite shapes. Arrange them attractively on the sheet of cardboard and trace around them with the pencil or felt-tip pen. Set aside the paper shapes.

5. Cut your colored paper into many small pieces—circles, diamonds, triangles, squiggly shapes.
6. Touch a dab of glue or rubber cement to the back of a piece from step 5 and apply it to part of your design. Continue doing this until you fill in the design with your colored mosaic pieces.

WINDOW SHADE PICTURE

When there's no sun to shine in the window, pull this down for a big surprise!

You will need:

1. An old window shade, white or light-colored.
2. Poster or acrylic paints, crayons, India ink—all or any combination of these.
3. Paintbrushes, pens, and sponges.

What to do:

1. Lay the window shade flat on a large surface.
2. Make a colorful design or paint a vivid picture. Get as wild as you wish, for the shade will be rolled up in the daytime, and you'll not be looking at it 24 hours a day.
3. When paints and inks have dried, hang the shade up in your window and flash your colors! Or, if you prefer, hang it on the wall as a decoration.

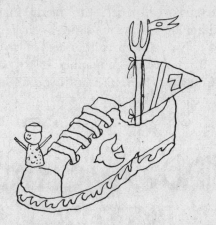

PAINTING OLD SHOES AND SNEAKERS

Go crazy with color—there's nothing to lose.
You're only decorating those old shoes!

You will need:

1. Old shoes or sneakers ready to be thrown out.
2. Newspaper.
3. Paints—acrylic, leftover house paint, anything not water-soluble—as many colors as you can find.
4. Felt-tip marking pens, and paintbrushes.
5. Water or turpentine to clean brushes and spills (see paint container for proper solvent).
6. Feathers, sequins, fancy buttons, any bits of junk you can scrounge around the house.
7. White household glue.

What to do:

1. Without soaking the shoes or sneakers, clean them the best you can or care to.
2. Stuff crumpled newspaper into the shoes so that they are firm enough to stand upright.
3. Decide on what designs or themes you want on the shoes, and pick your colors. You can mark designs on first with a marking pen if you want. Start painting.
4. Let the paint dry. Glue on your decorations. When this is dry, you have art objects for happy feet!

SPATTER PAINTING

Even a simple cutout design looks terrific when you spatter-paint it!

You will need:

1. Drawing paper.
2. Scissors and a pencil.
3. An old toothbrush.
4. Colored inks or poster paint, in shallow saucers so you can dip bristles of toothbrush.

What to do:

1. Make a stencil. Make up a simple design like a star, a leaf, or a boat, and draw it on a sheet of paper. Cut along the outline and discard the cutout piece. The remaining sheet is your stencil.

2. Lay a piece of drawing paper on your work surface and lay the stencil over it. Center the design and cover all but the open center cutout.

3. Dip the toothbrush bristles lightly, face down, into the paint or ink. Shake off any excess.

4. Hold the brush over the paper at the end nearer you. Hold the brush, bristles facing down, by the handle, with the head held away from you.

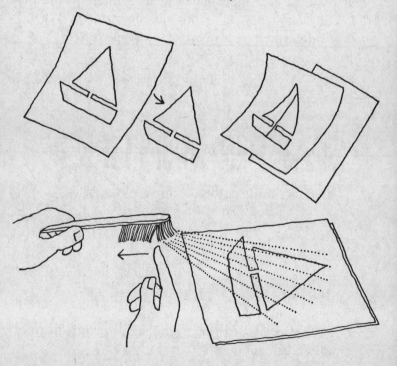

5. In a motion toward yourself, draw your finger lightly and briskly over the brush. A fine spray or spatter will fall over the paper.

6. Repeat step 5 until the cutout design is spattered evenly. If you like, you can clean off the toothbrush and dip it into a second color to get a two-toned effect.

7. When you've finished spattering, let the covering paper remain until the paint or ink is dry. Remove and behold your design!

8. Variation: Instead of using the stencil, use the piece that is cut out, and spatter around it, making a silhouette of solid color framed by spatter painting. Or do both: First spatter-paint the stencil, as in steps 1 to 6. When dry, spatter-paint the outside in a contrasting color.

ALUMINUM FOIL ENGRAVING

No muss, no fuss—a steady hand is what counts in this engraving project.

You will need:

1. Newspaper for padding.
2. A stiff piece of cardboard (such as a side cut from a carton box), about 9x12 inches.
3. Aluminum foil.
4. Cellophane tape.
5. A pencil and paper.
6. Engraving tools: a knitting needle, a large nail, the end of a spoon.

What to do:

1. Cut 6 pieces of newspaper to the size of the cardboard.
2. Tear off a sheet of aluminum foil large enough so that when folded double it will be 2 inches longer than the cardboard on all sides.
3. Set the pieces of newspaper on the cardboard.
4. Center the doubled foil over the top of the newspaper and fold back the edges of foil around the cardboard to the back. Turn over and crease the foil edges down flat. Tape to hold securely.
5. Turn the cardboard over so that the foil side faces you. Smooth out any wrinkles.

6. Plan your picture or design and draw it first on a piece of paper. Set it next to your foil to copy.
7. Press lightly with your engraving tool to avoid breaking through the foil. Use long, smooth strokes.
8. Try different engraving tools. Each one gives a different result.

WAX-ON-CANVAS PAINTING

Here's a fun way to use up those old candle stubs! You need to be very careful working with hot wax, but the results are super.

You will need:

1. A canvas on stretchers: 12x16 inches, or any standard size sold in art supply stores.
2. Stubs of old candles, a double boiler, a pot holder, and a trivet.
3. Poster paints, diluted, or water colors in tubes.
4. A large spoon.
5. A muffin tin or other container for mixing paints and water.
6. A paint rag.
7. A paintbrush about 1 inch wide.

What to do:

1. Lay the canvas on your work surface.

2. Put two or three 6-inch candles in the top of a double boiler and set over the water-filled bottom pan. Heat over medium heat until the candles melt. Careful! Melted wax is very hot. Use the pot holder to remove the pot from the stove. Set the pot on a trivet on your work surface.
3. With a large spoon, dribble the melted wax in squiggly lines up, down, and all around your canvas. Let dry for 15 minutes.
4. While the wax dries, mix your paints in the muffin tin or other containers. Mix 5 or 6 bright colors. Have a paint rag handy to clean the brush when switching from one color to another.
5. With the wax now dry and hard, brush on colors with large, bold strokes across the canvas. Let them overlap and run into each other. Cover the whole canvas with color. The wax background produces a tie-dyed look.

SCRATCH-OUT PAINTING

A stained-glass effect makes this a striking project for anyone who can handle a crayon!

You will need:

1. Wax crayons in black and various colors.
2. Heavy, smooth cardboard (oak tag or cardboard from a file folder is good).

3. A scratching tool (a comb, knife, crochet hook, or fork).

What to do:

1. Color the cardboard with all colors of crayons except black. Press hard and make a thick layer of color. Crayon in patches or stripes of color until the whole cardboard is colored.
2. Now color over the first layer with a thick layer of black crayon.
3. Scratch a picture or design through the black so that the lower layer of color shows through. It's beautiful!

PAPIER-MACHE BALLOON MASK

**This one's too good to wait for Halloween.
Get in on the fun right now.**

You will need:

1. A supply of old newspapers.
2. A round balloon.
3. Water.
4. A large pan.
5. Libray paste.
6. A paintbrush and paints.
7. Heavy yarn and white household glue.

What to do:

1. Tear the newspaper into strips 3 to 5 inches wide.
2. Soak the strips of paper in water. You can use a large sink.
3. Blow up the balloon so that it's about the size of your head. Knot or tie the end.
4. Gently squeeze the water from the paper. Tear it into smaller, easy-to-work strips and carry in the pan to your work area.
5. Apply the paste to the wet strips and paste them onto the balloon. Overlap the strips to cover the whole balloon. When you're through, there should be about 6 to 8 layers of newspaper strips.

6. Let the balloon mask dry about 24 hours or longer.
7. While waiting, practice designing mask faces.
8. When the mask is dry, paint your best face on it. After the paint dries, paste on lengths of yarn for hair.
9. Another time, instead of a mask, make a globe and paint in the continents and oceans.

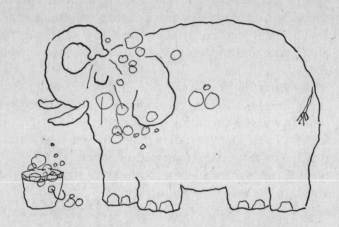

SOAP SCULPTURE

Different soaps for different folks!
See what you can come up with here.

You will need:

1. White bath soap.
2. Carving tools: a pocket knife, small kitchen knife, spoon, fork, large nail.
3. A pencil and paper.

What to do:

1. First, practice carving with your tools on a piece of soap until you get the hang of it.
2. Make a sketch, side view, of what you want to carve. Keep it simple. Try animal shapes (a bunny, cat, fish, or elephant), a boat, or a snowman.
3. With small, fine strokes, start tracing your outline on the wide side of the new piece of soap with the nail.
4. Using small cutting strokes, carefully start cutting along your outline, chipping out bits of soap as you go.
5. Work from the one broad side of the soap around to the other broad side, curving around the narrower sides to give a 3-dimensional look.
6. Work slowly. Don't make big cuts, or you might accidently cut away more than you intended.
7. Smooth off your sculpture with knife held at right angles to the soap for a finished effect.

Game Thing

Rajah

RAJAH

An intriguing game, easy to play and yet challenging to an expert player.

You will need:

1. An empty 12-egg carton.
2. Two small paper cups or muffin-tin liners.
3. Thirty-six dried beans (small buttons or paper clips may be substituted).
4. A friend to play with.

What to do:

1. Sitting opposite your opponent, set up the game as shown, the egg carton between the players and a paper cup at each end. The cup to the right of a player is his or her Home Cup.
2. Each player has 18 beans, and puts 3 into each carton-cup on his or her side. The Home Cup is left empty.
3. The players, A and B, will be moving beans in a clockwise direction from carton-cup to carton-cup. All

the beans contained in one carton-cup are moved at once; one bean is dropped into the next clockwise carton-cup, the second bean into the next, and so on, one bean at a time into successive carton-cups.

4. The object of the game is to get as many beans as you can into your Home Cup. There are two ways to get beans in the Home Cup. One, by having the last (only the last) bean in a play land at Home. Two, by capturing your opponent's beans.

5. During play, you may look into a carton-cup to get an idea of how many beans are in it, but you cannot touch them to count them. However, you can count beans in your Home Cup during your turn of play.

6. To begin play, the first player, A, takes the 3 beans

from any carton-cup on his or her side. Player A drops the first bean into the next clockwise cup, and so on, as described in step 3. Home Cups are not counted or used in play unless A's last bean would go into A's Home Cup (this cannot happen during the first play).

7. Depending on what carton-cup A's last bean goes into, one of three things will happen.

   a. If A's last bean is in a carton-cup on A's side, A captures all the beans inn the opposite carton-cup on B's side, and puts them into A's Home Cup. A's turn now ends.

   b. If A's last bean is in a carton-cup on B's side, A's turn ends without further action.

   c. If A's last bean ends at his or her own Home Cup (that is, if the next-to-last bean has gone into the carton-cup just short of Home Cup), A puts it in the Home Cup and takes another play.

8. The B player's turn follows the end of A's turn, and he or she plays the same way.

9. Turns alternate until one player wins.

10. One player wins when he or she gets 19 beans into the Home Cup, or if all the carton-cups on that player's side are empty at one time.

11. When you become expert players, you can add to the fun by starting the game with more beans in each carton-cup. Of course, the number of beans needed to win will be increased accordingly, to one more than half the total beans used.

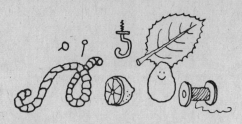

Plant Things

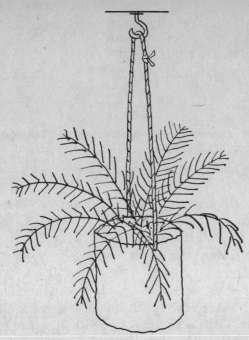

HANG A SPROUTING PLANT POT

**Hang up some pretty greenery
to brighten indoor scenery!**

You will need:

1. Several plastic foam sponges.
2. A plastic-laminated paper bucket, the kind painters use, or a take-out food carton or round ice-cream carton.
3. A screwdriver and scissors.

4. The leafy branches of a plant.
5. Thin rope, 4 to 6 feet long.
6. A long screw-in hook.

What to do:

1. Dip the sponges in water and squeeze enough water out to avoid having them drip.
2. Fill the bucket with sponges—loosely, not packed too tightly.
3. With a screwdriver, poke a hole through the bucket and into the sponges. Stick a branch well into the hole so it won't fall out.
4. Repeat step 3 until the bucket is covered with branches.
5. Poke 2 holes opposite each other near the top of the bucket. Thread the rope through the holes to form a big loop. Cut the rope to the desired length for hanging, and knot the ends together.
6. Screw the hook into the wall, ceiling, or woodwork in a light spot in the room. Hang the pot by the rope.
7. Plant hints: Some plants, like a Swedish ivy plant or a philodendron, will sprout roots and grow new leaves. Others will live quite a while in the sponge and then need replacing. For a lovely Christmas hanging, use small evergreen branches; they will stay green and fresh for the whole holiday season.
8. Keep the sponges moist by frequent watering.

LOAF PANS MAKE PRETTY PLANTERS

Why settle on ordinary flower pots when
you can make and decorate your own planter?

You will need:

1. Four wooden beads, from a notions store,
   an old necklace, or a baby toy.
2. A metal loaf pan.
3. White household glue.
4. Enamel paint in several colors.
5. Paintbrushes and brush cleaner (turpentine).
6. Gravel and potting soil.
7. A small plant.

What to do:

1. Glue a bead to each corner of the pan and let dry.
2. Paint the outside of the pan and let it dry.

3. To decorate the pan, paint flowers or birds on it, a design, a monogram, or your name. Again, let dry.
4. Put a layer of gravel in the pan for drainage. Fill with potting soil. Plant the plant and water thoroughly, but do not make the soil soggy.

ORGANIC GARDENING IN A CAN

You can make your own potting soil with a miniature compost pile.

You will need:

1. A 2-pound coffee can with a plastic lid.
2. Coffee grounds.
3. Newspapers.
4. Vegetable and fruit leavings: orange and apple peels, dried leaves, carrot scrapings, and what-have-you.
5. Crushed dry cereal.
6. Scissors or a screwdriver for punching holes in the coffee-can lid.
7. An avocado pit, a carrot or pineapple top, a sweet potato, or any small plant.

What to do:

1. Into the coffee can, put the coffee grounds, shredded pieces of newspaper, fruit and vegetable leavings, and

cereal. Everything should be broken into small pieces.

2. Stir the mixture well and moisten with water until everything is well dampened but not soggy.

3. Cover the can, poke several small holes in the top, and let it stand in a warm place for a week or so.

4. During this time, look inside each day. See if the mixture looks or smells different. Do you feel the can getting warmer? It should as the mixture begins to change into good compost.

5. When the week is up, stir the soil until it's well mixed.

6. Plant what you want to grow in the soil. Discard the lid of the can. Water as necessary and leave in a lighted spot on a windowsill or near a window.

7. Planting tips: An avocado pit can be sprouted in water first, or stick the heavy end into the soil, leaving the upper half exposed, and water daily for several weeks until it sprouts. Bury a carrot or pineapple top up to the stem section.

Things to Do When You're Sick in Bed

Fat Cat from an Old Pillowcase

Paper-Clip Necklace

Vegetable People

FAT CAT FROM AN OLD PILLOWCASE

**You'll wonder how you ever got along
without this fat cat pillow.**

You will need:

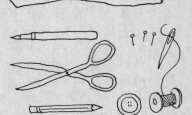

1. An old pillowcase.
2. A felt-tip pen.
3. Scissors and straight pins.
4. A needle and strong thread.
5. Cotton wool, kapok, or an old limp bed pillow for stuffing.
6. A pencil or knitting needle.
7. Felt scraps or buttons for eyes and nose.

What to do:

1. Turn the pillowcase wrong side out.

2. With the pen, draw an outline of a cat's head on one side of the pillowcase. Fit the ears into the corners. Make the head as large as possible.

3. Draw a second outline ½ inch inside the first outline. The inner line will be your sewing guide.

4. Cut out on the outer line. Pin the 2 pieces together. One will be the face, and the other the back of the cat's head. Sew along the remaining outline except for a space at the bottom that you'll need for stuffing.

5. Turn the cat right side out.

6. Stuff with whatever filling you have. You may need a pencil or knitting needle to poke the stuffing into the corners of the ears. If using an old pillow, squeeze and poke it into place.
7. Tuck inside the edges of the stuffing gap. Pin and sew.
8. Sew felt pieces or buttons for the eyes and nose. Touch up the eyes and draw the cat's whiskers with the pen.

PAPER-CLIP NECKLACE

**Link it, trim it—a for real, for a while,
and strictly for fun necklace.**

You will need:

1. Two to 3 dozen standard-size paper clips.
2. One-inch-wide cellophane tape in one or more colors, or colored gummed paper tape.
3. Scissors.

What to do:

1. Link the paper clips into a long chain.
2. Link the ends of the chain to make a necklace.
3. Cut a 1-inch piece of tape and wrap it around a paper-clip link, exactly in the middle of the clip. Leave only a tiny loop of the clip exposed at each end.
4. Repeat this step for the other links, using mixed and matched colors.

VEGETABLE PEOPLE

**Have fun making weird characters
to stand on your windowsill and cheer you up
when you're under the weather.**

You will need:

1. A few woody root vegetables: potatoes, carrots, turnips, beets.
2. Odds and ends to decorate your characters: thumbtacks, small cotton balls, yarn, fringe, scraps of felt and fabrics, Q-Tips, toothpicks, pipe cleaners, straight pins, and anything else you can think of.
3. White household glue.
4. India ink and a small paintbrush.

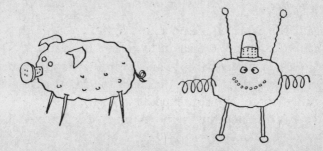

What to do:

1. Look at the illustrations for ideas for making people, animals, and out-of-this-world weirdos. Think of cartoons and space-age movies for inspiration.
2. Look over your odds and ends. A piece of purple fringe could be hair; Q-Tips for antenna eyes; toothpicks for legs; a thumbtack for a nose. Let your imagination go wild.
3. Experiment also with glued-on yarn for beards, felt ears, ribbon belts, bits of cloth for kerchief or skirt, pipe-cleaner arms.
4. Touch up with India ink; paint on whiskers; and add other features as your fancy dictates.
5. Your creations can be weird, or they can be cute and lovable, corny and comical. Anything goes.

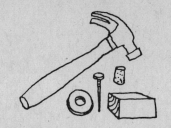

Things with Wood and Stuff

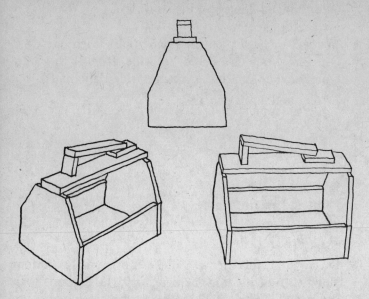

SHOESHINE BOX

**Here's a good wood project.
Why not paint Dad's initials on it
and make it a gift for him?**

You will need:

1. Pieces of wood ½-inch thick, cut into pieces these sizes:

    Two 9 inches long by 9½ inches wide
      (label each one *End*)
    One 12 inches long by 9½ inches wide
      (label it *Bottom*)
    Two 12 inches long by 3½ inches wide
      (label each one *Side*)

One 12 inches long by 4 inches wide
   (label it *Crosspiece*)
Three 2 inches by 2 inches wide (label each one *C*)
One 2 inches long by 8 inches wide (label it *E*)
One 2 inches long by 1½ inches wide (label it *D*)

2. A ruler and a soft pencil.
3. A saw.
4. Nails, 1½ inches long.
5. A hammer.
6. White household glue.
7. Sandpaper, coarse and fine.
8. Paint and a paintbrush.

What to do:

1. On an End, measure 4½ inches up from the bottom along each of the 9-inch sides. Mark the 2 points with the pencil. Label these marks *A*. Repeat this for the other End.

2. Along the top edge of an End, measure in 2¾ inches from each side and mark with pencil at both points. Repeat this for the other End. Label these marks *B*.

3. Using the ruler, draw a straight line between an A mark and the nearest B mark. Repeat, drawing a total of 2 diagonal lines on each End.

4. Saw along the diagonal lines on both Ends (ask an adult for help if you haven't had much experience with a saw). Discard the small triangles of wood you've cut off.

5. Nail an End to the Bottom, matching up the 9½-inch edge of the End to the 9½-inch edge of the Bottom. Set the pieces at right angles to each other, with End overlapping the Bottom. You will nail through the End into the Bottom.

6. Nail the second End to the Bottom the same way, on the opposite edge of the Bottom.

7. Set your U-shaped structure on one end. Place a Side piece on its long edge along the edge of the Bottom. The Side's two ends will fit between the Ends. Nail through the top End into the Side. Turn the whole thing over and nail the other End into the Side. Next, turn so that the Bottom is up, and nail from the Bottom into the Side.

8. Repeat step 7 for the second Side piece.

9. Turning the shoeshine box on one End again, fit the Crosspiece into place at the top of the End pieces, similar to the way you fitted the Sides between the Ends. Nail the Ends into the Crosspiece similarly.

10. With the basic structure built, you will add the shoe rest. First the toe piece: Glue 2 pieces marked C together. Glue this block to the Crosspiece, about $1\frac{1}{2}$ inches from an end, and centered side to side. Let the glue dry, and hammer in one nail for extra security.

11. Set the E piece on the Crosspiece, one end resting on top of the C block, overlapping it by about $\frac{1}{2}$ inch. The other end of E will slant downhill onto the Crosspiece itself. Glue both ends of E and set it in place to dry.

12. Set the remaining C piece on the Crosspiece, butting it against the lower edge of E. Glue it into place. When dry, secure with one nail.

13. Set the D piece on top of the C block and butt it against the upper end of E. Glue it in place.

14. When all is dry, check over the shoeshine box for protruding nail ends, and hammer them over flat against the wood.

15. Sand the rough edges of the wood with coarse sandpaper. Sand the entire shoeshine box with fine sandpaper. Clean it off thoroughly, finishing with a damp rag. If dust remains, it will make a poor paint job.
16. Paint the shoeshine box, following the directions on the paint can. You'll probably need 2 coats of paint.

BOTTLE-CAP MOBILE

Smiles galore on this mobile—just what you need to brighten your room!

You will need:

1. Eighteen soda-bottle caps.
2. Model airplane enamel, light and

dark colors, and small paintbrushes.

3. Fine cord or heavy sewing thread.
4. A roll of plastic mending tape.
5. A small amount of modeling clay.
6. White household glue.
7. A small nail and a hammer.
8. The plastic lid from a 2-pound
   can of coffee, or a circle of ply-
   wood cut to the same size.
9. Scissors.
10. (Optional, for hanging) a screw-
    eye.

What to do:

1. Paint the outside of the bottle caps, some with dark
   colors and others with light colors, in a color scheme
   you like. Let the paint dry.
2. Paint a wide smile and two dots for eyes on each
   bottle cap. Use contrasting colors. Let dry.

3. Cut 9 pieces of cord in these lengths: 27, 23, 18, 16,
   12, 9, 6, and 3 inches.
4. Tie a knot in the end of each cord. Tape each knot to
   the inside of a cap so that the cord comes out at the
   top of a face.
5. Roll a small ball of modeling clay. The clay ball's
   diameter should be about twice the depth of a bottle

cap. Set the ball of clay on top of the knot and tape inside one bottle cap.

6. Roll 8 more balls of clay and repeat step 5 with the 8 remaining cord-taped caps.

7. Put glue around the edges of one of these caps. Now take one of your so-far-unused caps (no cord attached) and set it over the first cap, edge to edge, inner sides facing. Be sure the cord emerges at the top of the face of the added cap. Press together and hold firmly a minute or two.

8. Repeat step 7 for the rest of the caps.

9. With the nail and hammer, punch holes in the coffee can lid as shown in the illustration.

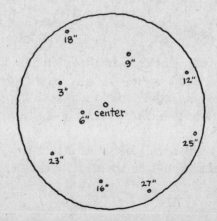

10. Line up the smiles by the lengths of their cords. Pull the loose cord ends through holes in the lid. Follow the diagram, putting the 6-inch cord through the hole marked 6 inches, and so on. Tie a bulky knot at the end of each cord so that it won't pull through the hole.

11. Cut another piece of cord about 6 inches long. Knot one end and draw the other end through the center hole of the lid.

12. Tie the other end of this hanging cord to a lamp, to a screweye at the top of a doorway, or to some other spot where there is a slight movement of air.

TOTEM POLE

This is an activity borrowed from the American Indians. It could make an interesting school project also.

You will need:

1. Pieces of leftover lumber. (Ask at your local lumberyard; salvage scraps from handyman projects at home and from neighbors; and scrounge some pieces from the building blocks you used to play with.)

2. White household glue.

3. Sandpaper.

4. Poster paint or interior wall paint, assorted bright colors and black.

5. Paintbrushes, small and medium sizes.

What to do:

1. Spread the wood pieces out on your working surface and see how they might go together. A bigger piece at the bottom, an angled piece here, a short dowel there; mix them up, sort them out, try different pieces together.

2. Begin gluing pieces together, starting at the bottom. Provide a solid base and put heavier pieces near the bottom. Glue as you go. Let one glue application dry before attaching another piece.

3. When the totem pole is completed and thoroughly dry, sand it smooth. Remove all dust before painting. End up wiping it with a damp rag.

130

4. Start painting. Big mouths and eyes and exaggerated features will add to the totem-pole look. Remember to let the paint dry thoroughly before adding another color, so that you get clean, sharp edges instead of blurry smears.

HOW TO MAKE A CRICKET CAGE

In the Oriental tradition, a cricket brings
a home good luck—and makes
a problem-free pet!

You will need:

1. Two pieces of cardboard, about 3 inches square, cut from a corrugated cardboard box.
2. A small hammer and a small nail, about toothpick size.
3. A box of round wooden toothpicks.
4. White household glue.

What to do:

1. Make a sandwich of the cardboard squares, lining them up edge to edge.
2. With nail and hammer, punch holes ¼ inch apart around the outside edges, ¼ inch in from the edge. Do this through both layers of cardboard at the same time, so the pieces will have matching holes.
3. Insert the toothpicks through both pieces of cardboard.
4. Gently pull the pieces of cardboard apart, sliding them up or down on the toothpicks, so that one forms the floor and the other the roof of the cage.

132

5. Place a dab of glue on each spot where a toothpick meets cardboard, to hold the cage together. Before doing this, read the next step!

6. Leave 2 adjacent toothpicks unglued so that your cage has a door to lift up when putting in a cricket.
7. Whether you actually keep a cricket or not, you have a little box with a secret door to keep tiny treasures in. You can leave a few more toothpicks unglued, depending on how big your treasures are.

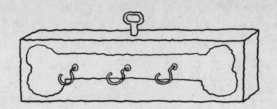

MAKE YOUR DOG A GIFT

Handy for you, too, so you know where your dog's belongings are!

You will need:

1. Sandpaper.
2. A piece of wood about 10 inches long, 4 inches wide, and ½ inch thick.
3. A soft pencil.
4. Poster paints and brushes.
5. Three screw cup hooks.
6. A picture ring, from a hardware store.

What to do:

1. Sand the wood until it is smooth. Wipe it clean of dust.
2. Draw a picture on the wood—something your dog likes. It could be a bone, a hot dog, a favorite toy. Or you could make a blue-ribbon bow to show that your pet is a real winner.

3. Paint the picture and let it dry.
4. Screw in the cup hooks, across the center in a row, about 2 or 3 inches apart.
5. Screw in the picture ring at the center top.
6. Hang it up in a convenient spot, and use it to hang up your dog's leash, brush, or comb, or whatever your dog needs.

Joan Eckstein and Joyce Gleit have collaborated on a few books for Avon previous to *Fun with Making Things—Fun with Growing Things, Fun in the Kitchen,* and *The Best Joke Books for Kids.* They are currently working on a new book, *A Loving Story.* Joan Eckstein lives in Brooklyn Heights, New York, and is the mother of one child. Joyce Gleit lives in Larchmont, New York, and is the mother of three children.

Stan Tusan lives with his wife and two children in Walnut Creek, California. He has worked in a film animation studio, an advertising agency, and for five years as the art editor for *Children's Digest* magazine. He now makes his living as a free-lance illustrator.